Sixth Edition

Answer Key

FOR

mosaicos

SPANISH AS A WORLD LANGUAGE

JULIET FALCE-ROBINSON

University of California, Los Angeles

Adapted by

ANNE CALDERÓN

PEARSON

Boston   Columbus   Indianapolis   New York   San Francisco   Upper Saddle River
Amsterdam   Cape Town   Dubai   London   Madrid   Milan   Munich   Paris   Montréal   Toronto
Delhi   Mexico City   São Paulo   Sydney   Hong Kong   Seoul   Singapore   Taipei   Tokyo

Senior Acquisitions Editor: Tiziana Aime
Senior Digital Product Manager: Samantha Alducin
Development Editors: Anne Calderón, Lisa DeWaard, Scott Gravina
Director of Program Management: Lisa Iarkowski
Team Lead Program Management: Amber Mackey
Program Manager: Nancy Stevenson
Team Lead Project Managers: Melissa Feimer
Media Coordinator: Regina Rivera
Project Manager: Lynne Breitfeller
Project Manager: Jenna Gray, PreMediaGlobal

Senior Art Director: Kathryn Foot
Operations Manager: Mary Fischer
Operations Specialist: Roy Pickering
Editorial and Marketing Assistant: Millie Chapman
Editor in Chief: Bob Hemmer
Director of Market Development: Kristine Suárez
World Languages Consultants: Yesha Brill, Mellissa Yokell, Denise Miller

This book was set in Sabon 10 pts.

10 9 8 7 6 5 4 3

PEARSON

ISBN - 10: 0-205-25544-2
ISBN - 13: 978-0-205-25544-3

Answer Key

Capítulo Preliminar

OP-05

1. c **2.** b **3.** b

OP-06

1. d **2.** a **3.** e **4.** b **5.** c

OP-07

Answers will vary.

OP-08

1. formal **4.** informal
2. informal **5.** informal
3. formal

OP-09

1. informal **2.** formal **3.** informal

OP-10

1. usted **4.** tú
2. tú **5.** tú
3. usted

OP-11

1. Conversación 1 **4.** Conversación 1
2. Conversación 2 **5.** Conversación 2
3. Conversación 1

OP-12

1. Buenos días **4.** Buenas tardes
2. Buenas tardes **5.** Buenas noches
3. Buenos días **6.** Buenas tardes

OP-13

1. c **3.** a **5.** b
2. d **4.** f **6.** e

OP-14

1. a **3.** b
2. a **4.** c

OP-15

1. Regular **3.** muy bien **5.** Tomás
2. mal **4.** Pedro

OP-16

1. Perdón **4.** De nada
2. Por favor **5.** Con permiso / Perdón
3. Por favor **6.** Gracias

OP-17

Answers will vary.

OP-18

1. Hasta luego / Adiós **4.** Perdón
2. Con permiso / Perdón **5.** Hasta mañana
3. Gracias

OP-19

1. borrador **3.** cuaderno **5.** mochila
2. cesto **4.** silla

OP-20

1. mesa / la mesa / una mesa / escritorio / el escritorio / un escritorio
2. lápiz / el lápiz / un lápiz / lápices / los lápices / unos lápices
3. calculadora / la calculadora / una calculadora
4. bolígrafo / el bolígrafo / un bolígrafo
5. silla / la silla / una silla

OP-21

1. viernes / sábado **4.** jueves
2. lunes **5.** viernes
3. domingo

OP-22

1. b **3.** h **5.** g **7.** c
2. e **4.** f **6.** a **8.** d

OP-23

Answers will vary.

OP-24

1. miércoles
2. domingo
3. abril
4. julio
5. noviembre

OP-25

Answers will vary.

OP-26

Answers will vary.

OP-27

Answers will vary.

OP-28

Answers will vary.

OP-29

1. profesor
2. estudiante
3. profesor
4. estudiante
5. estudiante
6. estudiante
7. ambos

OP-30

1. d   **2.** a   **3.** b   **4.** c

OP-31

1. Repita, por favor
2. Más alto, por favor
3. No comprendo
4. No sé

OP-32

1. a   **2.** c   **3.** b   **4.** b

OP-33

1. Beatriz
2. Yolanda
3. X
4. Iñaki
5. Joaquín
6. Ignacio

OP-34

1. Antonio Banderas
2. Enrique Iglesias
3. Shakira
4. Salma Hayek

OP-35

Answers will vary.

OP-37

1. Falso
2. Cierto
3. Falso
4. No se menciona

OP-38

1. a   **2.** c   **3.** b   **4.** b

OP-39

Answers will vary.

OP-40

1. Cierto
2. Cierto
3. Falso
4. Cierto
5. No se menciona

OP-41

1. ambos
2. Felipe
3. Felipe
4. Carmen
5. ambos

OP-42

1. pesimista
2. tradicional
3. introvertido
4. nervioso
5. serio
6. paciente

OP-43

1. moderno
2. pasivo
3. generoso
4. creativo

OP-44

Answers will vary.

OP-46

1. b   **2.** c   **3.** c   **4.** a   **5.** b

OP-47

Answers will vary.

OP-49

1. d   **2.** e   **3.** b   **4.** a   **5.** c

OP-50

1. 777-8532/7778532
2. 527-3314/5273314
3. 622-0587/6220587
4. 332-9467/3329467
5. 353-2800/3532800

OP-51

1. once
2. trece
3. veintitrés
4. setenta y siete
5. treinta y cinco
6. veintidós
7. treinta y seis
8. cuarenta y seis

OP-53

1. e   2. d   3. a   4. b   5. c

OP-54

1. 8:20   3. 4:00   5. 7:30
2. 10:15   4. 8:50

OP-55

1. las nueve y media de la mañana / las nueve y treinta de la mañana
2. las cinco menos cuarto de la tarde / las cinco menos quince de la tarde / las cuatro y cuarenta y cinco de la tarde
3. las once de la mañana
4. las dos y media de la tarde / las dos y treinta de la tarde
5. las once menos veinte de la mañana / las diez y cuarenta de la mañana

OP-56

Answers will vary.

Capítulo 1

01-05

1. Cierto   4. Falso   6. Cierto
2. Falso   5. No se   7. Cierto
3. Falso   menciona   8. Falso

01-06

1. a   2. c   3. b   4. e   5. d

01-07

1. g   2. d   3. b   4. c   5. a

01-08

1. literatura   4. interesantes
2. librería   5. fácil
3. historia   6. biblioteca

01-09

1. a   2. c   3. b   4. a   5. d

01-10

1. no   4. en casa
2. baloncesto   5. en la cafetería
3. en la biblioteca   6. en la cafetería

01-11

Answers will vary.

01-12

Answers will vary.

01-13

Answers will vary.

01-14

1. estadística / la estadística
2. literatura / la literatura
3. periodismo / el periodismo

01-18

1. c   2. a   3. d   4. b   5. e

01-19

1, 4, 5, 6, 7

01-20

1. él / ella / usted   6. yo
2. yo   7. tú
3. ellos / ellas / ustedes   8. él / ella / usted
4. tú   9. ellos / ellas / ustedes
5. nosotros / nosotras

01-21

1. llega   4. trabaja
2. estudia   5. mira
3. escucha   6. baila

01-22

1. estudiamos   5. toma
2. monta   6. miro
3. bailan   7. practicamos
4. saca

01-23

Answers will vary.

01-25

1. profesor
2. los dos
3. los dos
4. los dos
5. estudiante
6. estudiante
7. profesor
8. los dos

01-26

1. viven
2. bebe
3. asisten
4. ven
5. comen

01-27

Answers will vary.

01-28

1. ___√___ hacer ejercicio
2. _____ ver una película
3. ___√___ tomar más agua
4. ___√___ ser más puntual
5. _____ caminar a la universidad
6. _____ llegar tarde a clase
7. _____ tomar café
8. ___√___ trabajar más

01-29

1. debo beber más agua
2. deben leer el libro de español
3. debemos correr por la mañana
4. debe asistir a clase todos los días

01-31

1. X
2. el
3. la
4. el
5. los
6. las
7. X

01-32

1. Yo tengo dos diccionarios / Tengo dos diccionarios
2. Yo tengo dos lápices / Tengo dos lápices
3. Yo tengo dos cuadernos / Tengo dos cuadernos
4. Yo tengo dos mochilas / Tengo dos mochilas
5. Yo tengo dos calculadoras / Tengo dos calculadoras

01-33

1. Necesita un bolígrafo
2. Necesitan un diccionario
3. Necesita una calculadora
4. Necesita una librería / Necesita ir a una librería
5. Necesitas una discoteca / Necesitas ir a una discoteca
6. Necesito un mapa
7. Necesita un televisor

01-34

1. lápices
2. bolígrafos
3. mochilas
4. cuadernos
5. mapas
6. calculadoras
7. cestos
8. papeles
9. libros
10. computadoras

01-35

1. Necesita cinco lápices
2. Necesita cinco bolígrafos
3. Necesita dos mochilas
4. Necesita cuatro cuadernos
5. Necesita tres mapas
6. Necesita dos calculadoras
7. Necesita un cesto
8. Necesita veinticinco papeles
9. Necesita ocho libros
10. Necesita una computadora

01-36

Answers will vary.

01-38

1. estás
2. Estoy
3. estás
4. Estoy
5. Estoy
6. está
7. está
8. están
9. estamos

01-39

1. Está en la biblioteca
2. Estás en la discoteca
3. Están en el restaurante
4. Están en el gimnasio
5. Estamos en la librería
6. Estoy en clase

01-40

1. f **2.** b **3.** c **4.** d **5.** e

01-41

Answers will vary.

01-42

1. Facultad de Ciencias
2. Gimnasio
3. Facultad de Medicina
4. Biblioteca
5. la librería / la Facultad de Humanidades, la Facultad de Humanidades / la librería

01-43

1. d **3.** c **5.** b **7.** a
2. f **4.** e **6.** g **8.** h

01-45

1. a **3.** a **5.** b **7.** c
2. a **4.** b **6.** b

01-46

Answers will vary.

01-47

Answers will vary.

01-51

Answers will vary.

01-52

4, 5

01-53

Answers will vary.

01-54

Answers will vary.

01-55

b

01-56

1. Falso
2. Falso
3. Falso
4. Cierto
5. Falso
6. No se menciona

01-57

Answers will vary.

01-58

Answers will vary.

01-60

1. e **2.** c **3.** a **4.** b **5.** d

01-61

1. c **2.** e **3.** b **4.** d **5.** a

01-62

1. b **2.** a **3.** d **4.** c

01-63

1. b **2.** a **3.** d **4.** c **5.** a

01-64

1. Falso
2. Falso
3. Falso
4. Cierto
5. Cierto

01-65

1. Cierto
2. Falso
3. No se menciona
4. Cierto
5. Falso

Capítulo 2

02-05

1. b **3.** b **5.** a **7.** b
2. a **4.** c **6.** a **8.** c

02-06

1. a **2.** b **3.** b **4.** d **5.** d **6.** b

02-07

Answers will vary.

02-08

1. b **2.** d **3.** e **4.** c **5.** a

02-09

1. Cierto
2. Falso
3. Cierto
4. No se menciona
5. Falso

02-10

1. Claudia
2. David
3. Ana
4. Ernesto

02-11

1. amarilla
2. verde
3. negra
4. blanca
5. marrón

02-12

1. puertorriqueño
2. venezolana
3. cubano
4. español
5. estadounidense / norteamericana / puertorriqueña
6. guatemalteca
7. mexicano
8. colombiano

02-13

Answers will vary.

02-14

1. mexicana
2. morena
3. español
4. fea
5. rojo
6. delgado

02-18

1. Ana
2. Ana
3. Ernesto y David
4. Ernesto
5. Ana o Ernesto
6. Ana
7. Ernesto y David
8. Ernesto

02-19

1. las profesoras
2. el profesor
3. los cuadernos
4. el estudiante
5. el laboratorio

02-20

1. colombianos
2. agradables
3. alegre
4. conversador
5. callada
6. simpática
7. lista
8. trabajadora
9. listo
10. perezoso

02-21

Answers will vary.

02-22

Answers will vary.

02-24

Answers will vary.

1. No se menciona
2. Cierto
3. Cierto
4. Falso
5. Cierto
6. Falso

02-25

1. es
2. son
3. soy
4. es
5. somos
6. eres

02-26

Answers will vary.

02-27

1. Es de la familia Alba / El televisor es de la familia Alba
2. Son de la profesora / Los libros son de la profesora
3. Es de Juan / La computadora es de Juan
4. Es de Susana / El teléfono es de Susana
5. Es de Pablo / El dinero es de Pablo

02-28

1. nueve / 9:00 / 9, noche
2. la biblioteca
3. el gimnasio
4. seis y media / 6:30

02-30

1. estás
2. Estoy
3. Es
4. Está
5. está
6. está
7. es

02-31

1. Está cansada
2. Está aburrida
3. Es trabajadora
4. Es inteligente
5. Está triste

02-32

1. es
2. es
3. son
4. estoy
5. es
6. es
7. somos
8. están
9. estoy
10. estoy

02-33

Answers will vary.

02-34

1. Estás   3. Estás   5. Estás
2. Son   4. Son   6. Eres

02-35

Answers will vary.

02-37

1. sus   4. tu   7. su
2. sus   5. nuestros
3. mi   6. sus

02-38

1. mi   4. tu / nuestra
2. tu   5. tus / nuestros
3. sus   6. mi

02-39

Answers will vary.

02-40

Answers will vary.

02-41

1. sus   6. Mi
2. sus   7. nuestra / su / mi
3. sus   8. su
4. Sus   9. sus
5. sus

02-43

1. b   2. c   3. b   4. a   5. b   6. d

02-44

1. Me gustan las discotecas / No me gustan las discotecas
2. Me gusta la arquitectura colonial / No me gusta la arquitectura colonial
3. Me gustan las películas de Brad Pitt / No me gustan las películas de Brad Pitt
4. Me gusta estudiar / No me gusta estudiar
5. Me gusta cantar / No me gusta cantar

02-45

1. le gustan / no le gustan
2. le gusta / no le gusta
3. le gustan / no le gustan
4. les gusta / no les gusta
5. le gusta / no le gusta

02-46

Answers will vary.

02-50

Answers will vary.

02-51

1. argentino   4. veintidós / 22
2. rubio   5. simpático
3. psicología   6. inteligente

02-52

Answers will vary.

02-53

Answers will vary.

02-54

Answers will vary.

02-55

1. Cierto   4. Falso
2. No se menciona 5. Cierto
3. Cierto

02-56

Answers will vary.

02-57

1. C   5. ambos
2. A   6. A
3. C   7. A
4. C

02-58

Answers will vary.

02-59

Answers will vary.

02-61

1. fuerte   3. alegre   5. pobre
2. rica   4. casados

02-62

1. delgada   4. bonita
2. listo / inteligente 5. simpático
3. perezoso

02-63

Answers will vary.

02-64

1. No se menciona   4. Falso
2. Cierto   5. Falso
3. Cierto

02-65

1. ambos   3. Claudia   5. Claudia
2. David   4. David

Capítulo 3

03-05

1. Cierto   7. Falso
2. Cierto   8. Falso
3. No se menciona   9. Cierto
4. Cierto   10. No se menciona
5. Falso   11. Cierto
6. Falso   12. Cierto

03-06

1. a   4. d   7. a   10. c   13. d
2. c   5. d   8. c   11. a   14. c
3. b   6. b   9. a   12. a

03-07

1. ver televisión, conversar en la computadora
2. ir al cine, bailar en la discoteca, leer revistas
3. escuchar música, tocar la guitarra, tomar algo en un café

03-08

Answers will vary.

03-09

Answers will vary.

03-10

1. e   2. b   3. c   4. d   5. a

03-11

Selected items: agua mineral, cereal, chocolate, helado, huevos, leche, lechuga, tomate

03-12

1. d   2. e   3. c   4. b   5. a

03-13

1. d   2. e   3. c   4. a   5. b

03-14

Horizontales:	Verticales:
4. queso	1. cerveza
5. sopa	2. vino
6. ensalada	3. pescado
8. tomate	7. sándwich
10. helado	8. té
11. jugo	9. agua
12. cereal	

03-18

1. salen   5. pongo   9. trae
2. pone   6. Salgo   10. ponemos
3. oye   7. hago
4. hace   8. oye / pone

03-19

Answers will vary.

03-20

1. hago ejercicio   4. traigo vino
2. oigo música   5. pongo flores
3. pongo la mesa   6. salgo

03-21

1. oye   4. pone, trae
2. hace   5. sale
3. hace

03-22

1. Yo hago la cama también / Hago la cama también
2. Yo preparo el desayuno también / Preparo el desayuno también

3. Yo traigo el periódico también / Traigo el periódico también

4. Yo salgo a comprar la comida también / Yo salgo a comprarla también / Salgo a comprar la comida también / Salgo a comprarla también

6. Voy a la playa / Vas a la playa / Yo voy a la playa / Tú vas a la playa

03-30

Answers will vary.

03-31

Answers will vary.

03-24

1. Cuzco   **3.** Arequipa   **5.** Lima

2. Iquitos   **4.** Ica

03-33

Teresa

03-25

1. c   **2.** a   **3.** e   **4.** b   **5.** d

03-34

1. 287   **3.** 213   **5.** 1000

2. 504   **4.** 704

03-26

1. va a la librería

2. van al supermercado

3. vas a la universidad

4. vamos a la cafetería

5. vas al cine

6. van a la residencia estudiantil

7. va a la discoteca

8. van a la playa

03-35

1. 189   **3.** 432   **5.** 533

2. 45   **4.** 271   **6.** 206

03-37

1. sabe   **3.** sabe   **5.** conoce

2. conoce   **4.** sabe

03-27

1. b   **2.** c   **3.** d   **4.** a   **5.** e

03-38

1. Conoces   **3.** sabe   **5.** sabe

2. Sabe   **4.** Conoces   **6.** saben

03-28

1. va a comprar un libro

2. vas a tomar una cerveza

3. van a ver una película

4. voy a descansar

5. van a tomar el sol

6. vamos a escuchar música

03-39

1. conoces   **4.** sé   **7.** conocer

2. conocer   **5.** Sabes

3. sabes   **6.** sabe

03-40

Answers will vary.

03-29

1. Voy a la librería / Vas a la librería / Yo voy a la librería / Tú vas a la librería

2. Van a la biblioteca / Los estudiantes van a la biblioteca / Ellos van a la biblioteca

3. Va al cine / El profesor va al cine / Él va al cine

4. Voy a la cafetería / Vas a la cafetería / Yo voy a la cafetería / Tú vas a la cafetería

5. Van a la discoteca / Mis amigos van a la discoteca / Tus amigos van a la discoteca / Ellos van a la discoteca

03-42

1. para   **2.** Por   **3.** por   **4.** por

03-43

1. Por   **3.** por   **5.** para   **7.** Por

2. por   **4.** Por   **6.** por   **8.** para

03-44

1. para   **3.** para   **5.** para

2. por   **4.** para   **6.** por

03-45

1. Por
2. para
3. para
4. para
5. por
6. por
7. por

03-49

Answers will vary.

03-50

1. b
2. a
3. c
4. b
5. c
6. c

03-51

Answers will vary.

03-52

Answers will vary.

03-53

1. b
2. a

03-54

1. Falso
2. Cierto
3. Cierto
4. Cierto
5. Falso
6. Cierto
7. No se menciona

03-55

Answers will vary.

03-56

Answers will vary.

03-57

Answers will vary.

03-58

1. c
2. f
3. a
4. b
5. e
6. d

03-60

1. d
2. e
3. b
4. c
5. a

03-61

Answers will vary.

03-62

1. Cierto
2. Falso
3. Falso
4. Cierto
5. Cierto
6. No se menciona

03-63

Answers will vary.

Capítulo 4

04-05

1. d
2. a
3. c
4. b

04-06

1. abuelo
2. primos
3. tío
4. madre / mamá
5. sobrina
6. nieto
7. hermanos
8. tía

04-07

1. Carmen
2. Jorge
3. Cristina
4. Carlos / Ricardo
5. Antonia / Laura
6. Gonzalo
7. Adolfo

04-08

1. padre, hijo
2. hermanos
3. esposos
4. hermanos
5. abuela, nieto

04-09

Answers will vary.

04-10

1. hermanastra
2. madrastra
3. esposo
4. nieta
5. tía

04-11

Answers will vary.

04-12

1. Cierto
2. No se menciona
3. Falso
4. Falso
5. Cierto
6. No se menciona
7. Falso

04-13

1. serio
2. Adolfo
3. madre / mamá
4. conversadora / divorciada

5. Andrés

6. padre, ocupado

7. Rosa

8. hermano

9. hermana

10. abuela, tranquila

04-14

1. c **2.** d **3.** e **4.** b **5.** a

04-18

1. a **3.** c **5.** d **7.** b

2. d **4.** b **6.** e **8.** a

04-19

1. Estados Unidos **4.** Estados Unidos

2. Estados Unidos **5.** ambos

3. Colombia

04-20

1. pueden **5.** cuestan

2. duermo **6.** juego

3. tengo **7.** juegan

4. vienen, vengo

04-21

1. dicen **4.** pido **7.** quiere

2. pienso **5.** Prefiero **8.** prefiere

3. quiero **6.** duerme

04-22

1. no puede **4.** no puede

2. no puede **5.** no pueden

3. pueden

04-24

1. Adolfo **4.** Julieta **7.** ambos

2. Julieta **5.** Julieta

3. Adolfo **6.** Adolfo

04-25

1. nos **3.** se **5.** se **7.** me **9.** nos

2. me **4.** se **6.** me **8.** se **10.** te

04-26

1. te levantas **3.** te vistes **5.** te lavas

2. te bañas **4.** te acuestas

04-27

1. se levanta **3.** se viste **5.** se duerme

2. se ducha **4.** se acuesta

04-28

Answers will vary.

04-30

1. tiene que **4.** Tengo que

2. Tienen que **5.** tienes que

3. tenemos que

04-31

1. tienes que hacer ejercicio

2. tienes que sacar tu pasaporte

3. tienen que practicar más

4. tienen que comprar unas canciones en iTunes

5. tienes que hablar con tu compañero

04-32

Answers will vary.

04-33

Answers will vary.

04-35

1. cuatro años / 4 años **3.** un año / 1 año

2. dos años / 2 años **4.** tres meses / 3 meses

04-36

1. Hace tres años que mi hermana juega al voleibol

2. Hace un año que estudio español

3. Hace diez años que mis padres viven en nuestra casa

4. ¿Cuánto tiempo hace que tienes tu coche nuevo?

5. Hace tres años que tengo mi coche nuevo

04-37

Answers will vary.

04-41

1. 9:00 / 9 **2.** 2:00 / 2 **3.** 3:00 / 3

04-42

1. clase de inglés

2. clase de economía

3. examen de sociología

4. nada

5. fiesta

6. nada

04-43

1. Museo

2. 16 / dieciséis

3. 5 / cinco

04-44

Answers will vary.

04-45

1. c

04-46

1. Falso **5.** Cierto

2. Falso **6.** Cierto

3. No se menciona **7.** Falso

4. No se menciona **8.** Falso

04-47

Answers will vary.

04-48

Answers will vary.

04-49

Answers will vary.

04-51

Answers will vary.

04-52

Answers will vary.

04-53

1. a **2.** c **3.** b **4.** a **5.** b

04-54

1. Cierto **5.** Falso

2. No se menciona **6.** Falso

3. No se menciona **7.** Cierto

4. Cierto

Capítulo 5

05-05

1. a **2.** b **3.** d **4.** e **5.** c

05-06

1. muebles **5.** lavaplatos

2. cama **6.** lavabo

3. sofá **7.** chimenea

4. refrigerador **8.** piscina

05-07

1. pequeña **5.** la cocina

2. bonita **6.** la sala

3. un **7.** flores

4. dos **8.** la piscina

05-08

1. c **2.** a **3.** d **4.** e **5.** b

05-09

1. Cierto **5.** No se menciona

2. Falso **6.** No se menciona

3. No se menciona **7.** Falso

4. Falso **8.** No se menciona

05-10

Answers will vary.

05-11

Answers will vary.

05-12

1. j **3.** d **5.** a **7.** f **9.** g

2. b **4.** i **6.** e **8.** h **10.** c

05-13

1. b **2.** b **3.** a **4.** a **5.** b **6.** c

05-17

1. b   **2.** c   **3.** a   **4.** c   **5.** a   **6.** b

05-18

1. c   **2.** b   **3.** a   **4.** d   **5.** e

05-19

1. está cortando

2. está limpiando

3. está barriendo

4. está pasando

5. está haciendo

05-20

Answers will vary.

05-21

1. Papá está mirando la televisión

2. Clara está sacando la basura

3. Luis está estudiando

4. Pablo está leyendo un libro

5. El abuelo está escuchando la radio

6. El perro está durmiendo en la sala

05-22

Answers will vary.

05-24

1. Tiene sueño   **4.** Tiene miedo

2. Tiene frío   **5.** Tiene hambre

3. Tiene prisa   **6.** Tienen calor

05-25

1. b   **2.** c   **3.** a   **4.** b   **5.** c

05-26

1. tiene sueño

2. tiene hambre

3. tienen miedo / tienen cuidado

4. tiene prisa

5. tiene suerte

05-27

1. tiene sueño   **2.** tiene sed   **3.** tiene razón

05-28

Answers will vary.

05-30

1. Las   **3.** La   **5.** Lo   **7.** Las

2. Los   **4.** La   **6.** Lo

05-31

1. d   **2.** c   **3.** e   **4.** b   **5.** a

05-32

1. d   **2.** b   **3.** c   **4.** a   **5.** a

05-33

1. a   **2.** d   **3.** b   **4.** c   **5.** b

05-34

Answers may vary.

05-35

Answers may vary.

05-36

1. su madre / mi madre / la madre / madre

2. su hermano / mi hermano / el hermano / hermano

3. sus hermanas gemelas / sus hermanas / mis hermanas gemelas / mis hermanas / hermanas gemelas / hermanas

4. sus abuelos / mis abuelos / los abuelos / abuelos

5. su abuela / mi abuela / la abuela / abuela

05-38

1. este   **4.** esa / aquella   **7.** este

2. aquel / ese   **5.** estos   **8.** Ese

3. estas   **6.** Ese / Aquel

05-39

1. eso   **3.** aquello   **5.** Eso / Esto

2. Esto   **4.** esto

05-40

1. ese / aquel   **3.** estos / esos   **5.** este

2. esta   **4.** aquellas

05-41

1. b   **2.** a   **3.** c   **4.** b   **5.** d

05-45

Answers will vary.

05-46

1. Cierto
2. Falso
3. Falso
4. Cierto
5. No se menciona
6. Cierto

05-47

Answers will vary.

05-48

Answers will vary.

05-49

1. No
2. No
3. Sí
4. Sí
5. Sí
6. No
7. No
8. Sí

05-50

1. Falso
2. No se menciona
3. Cierto
4. Falso
5. Cierto
6. No se menciona

05-51

Answers will vary.

05-52

Answers will vary.

05-53

Answers will vary.

05-54

Answers will vary.

05-56

Answers will vary.

05-57

1. No se menciona
2. No se menciona
3. Jaime
4. Jaime + otros

05-58

1. Cierto
2. Falso
3. No se menciona
4. Falso
5. Cierto
6. No se menciona
7. Cierto

Capítulo 6

06-05

1. b
2. a
3. c
4. b
5. c

06-06

1. b
2. e
3. d
4. a
5. c

06-07

1. e
2. d
3. b
4. a
5. c

06-08

1. e
2. d
3. b
4. a
5. c

06-09

1. c
2. a
3. c
4. c
5. a
6. a

06-10

1. Jorge
2. nadie
3. Ricardo
4. Alejandra
5. Ricardo
6. Alejandra
7. Jorge
8. Jorge
9. Ricardo
10. nadie
11. Alejandra
12. nadie
13. Alejandra

06-11

Answers will vary.

06-12

1. b
2. b
3. c
4. d
5. a
6. a
7. d
8. b
9. b
10. c
11. b
12. c

06-13

1. a
2. b
3. c
4. b
5. a
6. a
7. b

06-14

1. los pantalones
2. la bufanda
3. los guantes
4. el suéter de lana / el suéter
5. el abrigo

06-18

1. pasado
2. presente
3. pasado
4. presente

5. ambiguo   **7.** pasado

6. pasado   **8.** pasado

06-19

1. d   **3.** a   **5.** c   **7.** c

2. b   **4.** d   **6.** a

06-20

1. comí, hablé   **3.** miré, estudié

2. jugaron, comieron   **4.** asistieron, tomaron

06-21

1. Diana   **5.** Diana

2. Jorge   **6.** Jorge

3. ambos   **7.** ambos

4. Jorge   **8.** Jorge

06-22

1. a   **3.** b   **5.** c   **7.** d

2. e   **4.** c   **6.** b   **8.** a

06-23

Answers will vary.

06-24

1. Llegó a las dos / El hombre llegó a las dos / Él llegó a las dos

2. Los dependientes hablaron con él

3. Miró los collares / Él miró los collares

4. Salió rápidamente de la tienda / Salió de la tienda rápidamente / El hombre salió rápidamente de la tienda / El hombre salió rápidamente / Salió rápidamente / El hombre salió de la tienda rápidamente

5. Llamé a la policía / Yo llamé a la policía

06-26

1. fueron   **6.** fuimos

2. fuimos   **7.** fue

3. fuimos   **8.** fuimos

4. fue   **9.** fuimos

5. fue   **10.** Fueron

06-27

Answers will vary.

06-28

1. ir   **3.** ir   **5.** ser

2. ser   **4.** ser   **6.** ir

06-29

1. Fue   **3.** fueron   **5.** fue

2. fue   **4.** fueron

06-30

Answers will vary.

06-32

1. les   **2.** le   **3.** le   **4.** les   **5.** les

06-33

1. Sí, le compré un paraguas

2. Sí, les compré unas bufandas

3. Sí, le compré unos zapatos de tenis

4. Sí, le compré unas pulseras

5. Sí, te compré algo interesante

06-34

Answers may vary.

06-35

Answers may vary.

06-37

1. c   **2.** a   **3.** c   **4.** c   **5.** a

06-38

Answers will vary.

06-39

1. gustó   **4.** cayó

2. gustaron   **5.** interesan

3. parecieron   **6.** encantó

06-40

Selected items: los estudios; la biología; conversar con los amigos; hablar de la política; la música popular; la música rock, bailar

06-41

Answers will vary.

06-43

1. es
2. Es
3. es
4. es
5. está
6. está
7. está

06-44

Answers will vary.

06-45

1. es
2. es
3. es
4. es
5. está
6. estoy
7. es
8. ser

06-49

Answers will vary.

06-50

Answers will vary.

06-51

Answers may vary.

06-52

Answers will vary.

06-53

Answers will vary.

06-54

1. Falso
2. No se menciona
3. Cierto
4. Cierto
5. Falso
6. Falso
7. No se menciona
8. Falso

06-55

1. a   2. a   3. b

06-56

Answers will vary.

06-57

Answers will vary.

06-58

Answers will vary.

06-60

1. Cierto
2. Falso
3. Cierto
4. Falso
5. No se menciona
6. Cierto
7. No se menciona

06-61

1. c   2. c   3. c   4. b

Capítulo 7

07-05

1. el baloncesto / el básquetbol / baloncesto / básquetbol
2. el ciclismo / ciclismo
3. el golf / golf
4. el tenis / tenis
5. el fútbol / fútbol

07-06

1. c   2. a   3. d   4. e   5. b

07-07

1. raqueta
2. bate
3. palos
4. red
5. bate

07-08

1. el esquí
2. el tenis
3. el vóleibol
4. el ciclismo

07-09

Answers may vary.

07-10

Answers will vary.

07-11

1. b   2. a   3. b   4. c   5. b

07-12

1. a   2. d   3. b   4. f   5. e   6. c

07-13

1. c   2. a   3. b   4. d

07-14

1. esquí
2. tenis
3. ciclismo
4. vóleibol

07-15

1. b 2. a 3. c 4. d 5. d

07-16

1. campeonato
2. aficionados
3. equipo
4. se levantó
5. se puso
6. fue
7. ganó
8. jugadores

07-20

1. ambos
2. Gabriela
3. Franco
4. ambos
5. Franco
6. Franco
7. Gabriela
8. ambos

07-21

1. se despertó
2. se levantó
3. se bañó
4. se secó
5. se vistió
6. se lavó los dientes
7. se puso el camisón
8. se acostó

07-22

1. Se acostaron
2. se levantaron
3. Se pusieron
4. Se divirtieron
5. se fueron

07-23

1. se levantó
2. se bañó
3. se puso
4. se quedó
5. se acostó
6. se durmió

07-24

1. me levanté
2. nos pusimos
3. se lavó
4. me acosté

07-25

Answers will vary.

07-26

Answers will vary.

07-28

1. leyó
2. oyó
3. oyeron
4. leyó

07-29

1. Oíste
2. oí
3. creí
4. leí
5. leíste
6. leímos

07-30

Answers will vary.

07-32

1. tú
2. yo (Gabriela)
3. Franco y César
4. tú
5. yo (Gabriela)
6. Franco

07-33

1. se vistió
2. durmieron
3. prefirió
4. oyeron
5. pidieron

07-34

1. Franco repitió la buena noticia muchas veces
2. Ellos sirvieron cerveza para celebrar el triunfo / Ellos, para celebrar el triunfo, sirvieron cerveza
3. Gabriela prefirió tomar vino
4. César se vistió con los colores del equipo
5. Ellos no durmieron esa noche / Ellos esa noche no durmieron

07-35

Answers will vary.

07-37

1. Es para ella
2. Son para ellos
3. Es para él
4. Es para él
5. Son para ellas
6. Son para mí
7. Son para nosotras / Son para nosotros Son para mí y para ti / Son para ti y para mí

07-38

1. conmigo
2. con
3. sin
4. mí
5. ti
6. contigo
7. nosotros

07-39

1. ¿Contigo?
2. ¿De él?
3. ¿De mí?
4. ¿Sin ella?
5. ¿Para mí?
6. ¿Conmigo?

07-41

1. estuvo
2. vino
3. quiso
4. tradujo
5. tuvo
6. pudo

07-42

1. Fui al cine / No fui al cine / Yo fui al cine / Yo no fui al cine
2. Me puse ropa elegante / No me puse ropa elegante / Yo me puse ropa elegante / Yo no me puse ropa elegante
3. Quise ir a la playa / No quise ir a la playa / Yo quise ir a la playa / Yo no quise ir a la playa
4. Descansé / No descansé / Yo descansé / Yo no descansé
5. Hice la tarea / No hice la tarea / Yo hice la tarea / Yo no hice la tarea
6. Estuve en casa / No estuve en casa / Yo estuve en casa / Yo no estuve en casa
7. Me bañé / No me bañé / Yo me bañé / Yo no me bañé
8. Tuve mucho trabajo / No tuve mucho trabajo / Yo tuve mucho trabajo / Yo no tuve mucho trabajo

07-43

Answers may vary.

07-44

1. fuimos
2. estuvimos
3. vimos
4. Fue
5. tomamos
6. tuvimos
7. pudimos
8. nos pusimos

07-45

1. Pasó la aspiradora ayer / Gabriela pasó la aspiradora ayer / Ayer pasó la aspiradora / Ayer Gabriela pasó la aspiradora
2. Lavamos los platos ayer / Nosotros lavamos los platos ayer / Ayer lavamos los platos / Ayer nosotros lavamos los platos

3. Puso comida ayer / Franco puso comida ayer / Ayer puso comida / Ayer Franco puso comida
4. Hice la tarea de español ayer / Yo hice la tarea de español ayer / Ayer hice la tarea de español / Ayer yo hice la tarea de español
5. Fueron al supermercado ayer / Gabriela y Franco fueron al supermercado ayer / Franco y Gabriela fueron ayer al supermercado / Ayer fueron al supermercado / Ayer Gabriela y Franco fueron al supermercado / Ayer Franco y Gabriela fueron al supermercado

07-46

Answers will vary.

07-47

Answers will vary.

07-48

1. hace diez minutos
2. hace dos minutos
3. hace cuarenta minutos
4. hace quince minutos
5. hace veinticinco minutos
6. Sí, llegaron todos / Sí, todos llegaron / Sí
7. Santiago llegó primero / Santiago

07-52

Answers will vary.

07-53

1. a
2. b
3. a
4. c
5. a

07-54

Answers will vary.

07-55

Answers will vary.

07-56

1. b
2. b
3. c

07-57

1. Falso
2. Falso
3. Cierto
4. No se menciona
5. Falso
6. Cierto

07-62

1. a   **2.** b   **3.** b   **4.** c   **5.** c

07-63

Answers will vary.

07-64

1. b   **2.** b   **3.** c   **4.** b

Capítulo 8

08-05

1. c   **2.** a   **3.** d   **4.** e   **5.** b

08-06

1. f   **2.** e   **3.** a   **4.** b   **5.** c   **6.** d

08-07

1. d   **2.** c   **3.** a   **4.** e   **5.** b

08-08

1. e   **2.** a   **3.** d   **4.** c   **5.** b

08-09

1. b   **3.** c   **5.** a   **7.** c

2. a   **4.** c   **6.** c   **8.** b

08-10

1. la Navidad

2. el Día de la Madre

3. la Nochevieja

4. el Día de las Brujas

5. el Día de Acción de Gracias

08-11

Answers will vary.

08-12

1. Independencia   **5.** Nuevo

2. Navidad   **6.** Madre

3. Gracias   **7.** Pascua

4. Carnaval

08-13

1. invitación   **5.** ceremonia

2. boda   **6.** recepción

3. regalo   **7.** mariachis

4. compromiso   **8.** tradición

08-14

Answers will vary.

08-15

Answers will vary.

08-19

1. a   **2.** c   **3.** b   **4.** a   **5.** c   **6.** b

08-20

1. b   **2.** a   **3.** c   **4.** d

08-21

1. acción habitual

2. acción en progreso

3. descripción

4. descripción

5. acción habitual

08-22

1. b   **2.** c   **3.** d   **4.** a   **5.** b   **6.** a

08-23

1. Falso   **5.** Falso

2. Cierto   **6.** Cierto

3. Cierto   **7.** Cierto

4. No se menciona

08-24

1. íbamos   **5.** eran

2. nos reuníamos   **6.** jugábamos

3. cocinaba   **7.** estaba

4. miraba

08-25

Answers will vary.

08-27

1. b   **2.** a   **3.** c   **4.** a   **5.** b   **6.** a

08-28

1. a   **2.** c   **3.** b   **4.** a   **5.** b

08-29

1. habitualmente   **4.** una vez
2. habitualmente   **5.** una vez
3. habitualmente   **6.** una vez

08-30

Answers will vary.

08-32

1. más   **3.** más   **5.** más
2. menos   **4.** más

08-33

1. Cierto   **4.** Falso
2. Falso   **5.** No se sabe
3. Cierto

08-34

Answers will vary.

08-35

1. Hotel Miramar / Miramar
2. Hotel Miramar / Miramar
3. Hotel Sol / Sol
4. Hotel Trovador / Trovador
5. Hotel Trovador / Trovador
6. Hotel Sol / Sol

08-36

Answers will vary.

08-37

Answers will vary.

08-39

1. Falso   **3.** No se menciona
2. Falso   **4.** Cierto

5. Cierto   **7.** Falso
6. Cierto

08-40

1. tantas, como   **4.** tan, como
2. tanta, como   **5.** tantos, como
3. tan, como

08-41

1. tantos   **4.** tanto
2. tantos   **5.** tan
3. tantas   **6.** tan

08-42

1. Sí
2. No, Guillermo no es tan delgado como Héctor / No, Guillermo es menos delgado que Héctor / No, Héctor es más delgado que Guillermo
3. Sí
4. Sí
5. No, Héctor no tiene tantos zapatos como Guillermo / No, Héctor tiene menos zapatos que Guillermo / No, Guillermo tiene más zapatos que Héctor

08-44

1. la mejor   **4.** los mejores
2. fresquísimos   **5.** las más caras
3. buenísimo   **6.** grandísimas

08-45

1. Anita es la menor / Anita es la más joven
2. Ramón es el más alto
3. Raquel es la más baja
4. Ramón es el más pesado / Ramón pesa más
5. Raquel es la menos pesada / Raquel pesa menos
6. Raquel tiene la mejor condición física

08-46

1. Sí, el profesor de química es buenísimo / Sí, es buenísimo / Sí, él es buenísimo / El profesor de química es buenísimo / Es buenísimo / Él es buenísimo
2. Sí, nuestros compañeros son inteligentísimos / Sí, ellos son inteligentísimos / Sí, son inteligentísimos / Nuestros compañeros son

inteligentísimos / Ellos son inteligentísimos / Son inteligentísimos

3. Sí, la biblioteca es grandísima / Sí, es grandísima / La biblioteca es grandísima / Es grandísima

4. Sí, la comida de la cafetería es baratísima / Sí, la comida es baratísima / Sí, es baratísima / La comida de la cafetería es baratísima / La comida es baratísima / Es baratísima

5. Sí, la universidad es modernísima / Sí, es modernísima / La universidad es modernísima / Es modernísima

08-50

Answers will vary.

08-51

1. llegó, era
2. Vivió, se fue
3. se casó, tuvieron / tenían
4. celebraban, tenían
5. recibían

08-52

Answers will vary.

08-53

Answers will vary.

08-54

1. religiosa
2. religiosa
3. secular
4. secular
5. secular
6. religiosa
7. personal
8. secular
9. religiosa
10. secular
11. personal
12. secular
13. religiosa
14. religiosa

08-55

1. La Navidad / Navidad
2. El Día de los Santos Reyes / La Epifanía / El día de los Reyes Magos / El día de los Reyes
3. El 5 de Mayo / el cinco de Mayo / 5 de Mayo / cinco de Mayo
4. El 16 de septiembre / el dieciséis de septiembre / 16 de septiembre / dieciséis de septiembre
5. El 12 de diciembre / el doce de diciembre / 12 de diciembre / doce de diciembre

08-56

Answers will vary.

08-57

Answers will vary.

08-58

Answers will vary.

08-60

Answers will vary.

08-61

1. Cierto
2. Falso
3. No se menciona
4. Cierto
5. Falso
6. Falso

08-62

1. c   2. a   3. b   4. b   5. c

Capítulo 9

09-05

1. finca
2. cultivan
3. fuente de ingresos
4. bosque
5. madera
6. hierro

09-06

1. c   2. b   3. d   4. a   5. f   6. e

09-07

1. psicólogo
2. abogada
3. vendedor
4. actor
5. plomero / fontanero

09-08

1. i   3. f   5. d   7. h   9. j
2. b   4. e   6. g   8. a   10. c

09-09

1. bomberos
2. médico
3. abogada
4. policías
5. cocinero / chef
6. peluquera
7. locutores
8. periodistas
9. cajera

09-10

1. arquitecto   4. psicólogo   7. técnico
2. intérprete   5. médico
3. peluquero   6. abogado

09-11

1. cajera   4. actor
2. cocinero / chef   5. enfermera
3. policía

09-12

1. e   2. b   3. d   4. c   5. a

09-13

1. b   3. a   5. d   7. c
2. b   4. c   6. a

09-14

1. a   2. c   3. a   4. a   5. c

09-15

Answers will vary.

09-16

1. sueldo   4. empleado   7. vacante
2. solicitud   5. empresa
3. currículum   6. gerente

09-20

1. la   2. lo   3. la   4. los   5. lo

09-21

1. Cierto   4. Cierto
2. Falso   5. Cierto
3. No se menciona   6. Falso

09-22

1. objeto indirecto   5. objeto indirecto
2. objeto indirecto   6. objeto indirecto
3. objeto directo   7. objeto directo
4. objeto directo   8. objeto directo

09-24

1. te la   3. Te los   5. te la
2. Te lo   4. Te las

09-25

1. d   3. c   5. b
2. b   4. c   6. b

09-26

1. c   2. a   3. c   4. b   5. c

09-27

1. se lo compré / yo se lo compré
2. se las preparé / yo se las preparé
3. se las hice / yo se las hice
4. se lo llevé / yo se lo llevé
5. se los di / yo se los di

09-28

1. se la di a Alejandro   4. se lo di a Marta
2. te los di a ti   5. se las di a usted
3. se los di a ustedes

09-29

1. Alejandro se las da / Se las da Alejandro
2. Sandra se lo compra / Se lo compra Sandra
3. Marta se la regala / Se la regala Marta
4. Lorena se los regala / Se los regala Lorena

09-31

1. b   2. a   3. a   4. b   5. b

09-32

1. b   2. a   3. c   4. d   5. e

09-33

1. b   2. c   3. b   4. a   5. b

09-34

1. c   2. b   3. b   4. c

09-35

1. Eran   4. lloraba   7. podía
2. abrió   5. Entré   8. debía
3. dijo   6. estaba   9. podía

09-36

Answers will vary.

09-37

1. leía
2. llamó
3. preguntó
4. quería
5. dijo
6. tenía
7. Eran
8. llegó
9. fueron
10. cenaban
11. hablaban
12. se sentían

09-39

1. a   2. c   3. c   4. a   5. c

09-40

1. Lean
2. Visiten
3. Busquen
4. Envíen
5. Llenen
6. Vayan

09-41

1. Falso
2. Falso
3. Cierto
4. No se menciona
5. Falso
6. No se menciona
7. Cierto
8. Cierto

09-42

1. limpie
2. lave
3. saque
4. tenga
5. prepare

09-43

1. sean amables con los clientes
2. traigan las bebidas rápidamente
3. pongan la mesa correctamente
4. sirvan el agua frecuentemente
5. quiten los platos con cuidado

09-44

1. acéptela
2. llévelo
3. ábralas
4. recójalos
5. llévelos

09-45

Answers will vary.

09-46

Answers will vary.

09-50

Answers will vary.

09-51

Answers will vary.

09-52

Answers will vary.

09-53

Answers will vary.

09-54

Answers will vary.

09-55

Answers will vary.

09-56

Answers will vary.

09-57

Answers will vary.

09-58

Answers will vary.

09-60

1. c   2. a   3. a   4. a   5. c

09-61

1. c   2. a   3. a   4. b   5. c

09-62

Answers will vary.

Capítulo 10

10-05

1. b   2. e   3. c   4. a   5. f   6. d

10-06

1. c   2. d   3. a   4. d   5. c

10-07

1. la harina
2. el melón
3. el yogur
4. el aguacate
5. la langosta
6. el pastel
7. el aderezo

10-08

1. e   **2.** b   **3.** c   **4.** a   **5.** d

10-09

1. los campesinos
2. el maracuyá
3. una receta
4. el cordero
5. unas hierbas y especias

10-10

1. papaya
2. queso
3. dulces
4. mariscos
5. hierbas

10-11

1. f   **3.** e   **5.** b   **7.** a
2. d   **4.** g   **6.** h   **8.** c

10-12

Answers will vary.

10-13

Answers will vary.

10-14

1. b   **3.** a   **5.** b   **7.** d   **9.** a
2. c   **4.** d   **6.** b   **8.** d   **10.** a

10-15

1. la botella de vino / botella de vino / la botella / botella / el vino / vino
2. el vaso / vaso
3. la taza / taza
4. la cucharita / cucharita
5. la cuchara / cuchara
6. el cuchillo / cuchillo

7. el plato / plato
8. el tenedor / tenedor
9. la servilleta / servilleta
10. el mantel / mantel

10-18

1. se baten
2. se agrega
3. se pone
4. se cocinan
5. Se sirven
6. se disfrutan

10-19

1. el mercado
2. la biblioteca
3. la cocina de un restaurante
4. la discoteca
5. la playa
6. el comedor de la casa

10-20

1. Se almuerza
2. Se prepara
3. Se sirve
4. Se añade
5. Se pone
6. Se lavan
7. Se beben
8. Se disfruta
9. Se come

10-21

1. Cierto
2. Falso
3. Falso
4. No se menciona
5. Cierto
6. Cierto

10-22

Answers will vary.

10-23

Answers will vary.

10-25

1. c   **2.** b   **3.** a   **4.** e   **5.** d

10-26

1. 5   **3.** 2   **5.** 6   **7.** 3   **9.** 4
2. 8   **4.** 9   **6.** 1   **8.** 10   **10.** 7

10-27

1. han participado
2. han tenido
3. ha hecho
4. ha sufrido
5. ha deseado
6. han sido

10-28

Answers will vary.

10-29

Answers will vary.

10-30

Answers will vary.

10-31

1. rotas
2. abiertas
3. desordenado
4. encendido

10-33

1. c   2. e   3. b   4. a   5. d

10-34

Selected items:

limpiar la cocina   cocinar la carne

ir al supermercado   hablar con tus invitados

poner la mesa   divertirse

10-35

1. b   2. a   3. b   4. b   5. c   6. c

10-36

1. Bebe
2. Come
3. comas
4. Haz
5. Evita
6. pongas
7. Ven
8. bebas

10-37

Answers will vary.

10-38

Answers will vary.

10-40

1. Cuándo te graduarás
2. Qué harás después de graduarte
3. Vivirás en Ecuador
4. Qué tipo de trabajo harás
5. Te casarás

10-41

1. todas (nosotras)
2. Lola
3. todas (nosotras)
4. tú

5. Mariana
6. Mariana
7. Lola

10-42

1. asistirá
2. prepararán
3. tendremos
4. haré
5. saldrá
6. iremos
7. descansaré

10-43

1. será
2. dependerá
3. estudiarás
4. empezarás
5. te casarás
6. tendrán
7. dará
8. ayudarás
9. harás

10-44

Answers will vary.

10-45

Answers will vary.

10-49

Answers will vary.

10-50

1. c   2. b   3. b   4. a   5. c   6. c

10-51

Answers will vary.

10-52

Answers will vary.

10-53

Answers will vary.

10-54

1. Cierto
2. No se menciona
3. Falso
4. Cierto
5. Cierto
6. Falso
7. Falso
8. No se menciona
9. Falso
10. Cierto

10-55

1. e   2. d   3. b   4. a   5. c

10-56

Answers will vary.

10-57

Answers will vary.

10-58

Answers will vary.

10-60

Answers will vary.

10-61

1. Falso
2. No se menciona
3. Falso
4. Cierto
5. Cierto
6. No se menciona
7. Cierto

10-62

1. b   2. b   3. c   4. b   5. b   6. c

Capítulo 11

11-05

1. f   3. e   5. g   7. b
2. c   4. a   6. d

11-06

1. d   2. b   3. e   4. a   5. f   6. c

11-07

Answers will vary.

11-08

1. h   3. b   5. j   7. c   9. g
2. a   4. e   6. d   8. f   10. i

11-09

1. la sangre / sangre
2. el estómago / estómago
3. las orejas / los oídos / orejas / oídos
4. los pulmones / pulmones
5. el cuello / cuello
6. la muñeca / muñeca
7. la rodilla / el tobillo / rodilla / tobillo
8. los ojos / ojos

11-10

1. b   3. d   5. e   7. a
2. h   4. f   6. g   8. c

11-11

1. a, c   3. g   5. h   7. b
2. d   4. e   6. a, c   8. f

11-12

1. la garganta   4. la cabeza
2. el estómago   5. las piernas
3. la nariz

11-13

1. el tobillo   3. catarro   5. el oído
2. el brazo   4. fiebre

11-14

1. e   2. b   3. a   4. d   5. c

11-15

1. b   2. a   3. c   4. a

11-16

1. el consultorio médico / la farmacia
2. el hospital
3. la farmacia
4. el hospital
5. el hospital
6. el consultorio médico
7. la farmacia

11-17

Answers will vary.

11-21

1. a   2. b   3. c   4. a   5. a

11-22

1. c   2. a   3. d   4. b   5. d

11-23

1. c   4. a   7. c
2. b   5. a   8. b
3. a   6. b

11-24

Answers will vary.

11-25

Answers will vary.

11-26

1. Quiero que mi hermana viaje a Europa con sus amigas
2. Deseo que mi prima consiga una beca para estudiar en México
3. Quiero que mi madre tenga buena salud
4. Deseo que mi mejor amiga se gradúe con honores
5. Espero que mi papá pueda jubilarse este año / Espero que mi papá se pueda jubilar este año

11-28

1. b 2. c 3. a 4. c 5. b 6. b

11-29

1. coma
2. hagas
3. tomen
4. fume
5. eviten
6. veas
7. sigan

11-30

1. se siente
2. duele
3. aconseja
4. haga
5. vayas
6. lleve
7. está
8. tome
9. descanse

11-31

Answers will vary.

11-32

Answers will vary.

11-34

1. b 2. c 3. a 4. c 5. b 6. b

11-35

1. nos divirtamos
2. gastemos
3. comamos
4. hagamos
5. vaya
6. limpiemos

11-36

Answers will vary.

11-37

1. c 3. f 5. g 7. d
2. e 4. b 6. a

11-38

Answers will vary.

11-39

Answers will vary.

11-40

1. b 2. a 3. b 4. a 5. a

11-41

1. El cinturón es para Irma / Es para Irma
2. Las pulseras son para Josefina / Son para Josefina
3. La cartera es para ti / Es para ti
4. El disco compacto es para Pablito / El disco es para Pablito / Es para Pablito
5. El reloj es para Ramiro / Es para Ramiro
6. El suéter es para mí / Es para mí

11-42

1. por
2. para
3. por
4. por
5. para
6. para

11-43

1. para
2. por
3. por
4. para
5. por
6. para
7. por
8. para
9. por
10. para
11. por
12. para

11-44

1. a 2. d 3. f 4. b 5. e 6. c

11-45

Answers will vary.

11-49

Answers will vary.

11-50

1. d 2. c 3. f 4. b 5. e 6. a

11-51

1. no caminar o correr
2. tomar aspirina
3. tomar antibióticos
4. tomar té con limón

11-52

Answers will vary.

11-53

Selected items: pescado, vitaminas, deportes, frutas

11-54

1. Cierto
2. No se menciona
3. Cierto
4. Cierto
5. No se menciona
6. Falso
7. Cierto
8. Falso

11-55

Answers will vary.

11-56

Answers will vary.

11-57

Answers will vary.

11-58

Answers will vary.

11-60

Answers will vary.

11-61

1. Falso
2. No se menciona
3. Cierto
4. Cierto
5. No se menciona
6. Falso
7. Falso

11-62

1. Cierto
2. Falso
3. No se menciona
4. Falso
5. Cierto

Capítulo 12

12-05

1. e   2. c   3. a   4. b   5. d

12-06

1. e   2. f   3. b   4. d   5. c   6. a

12-07

1. b   3. a   5. d   7. c
2. b   4. d   6. a   8. c

12-08

1. b   3. g   5. d   7. e
2. c   4. a   6. f

12-09

1. Falso   5. No se menciona
2. No se menciona   6. Cierto
3. Falso   7. Falso
4. Cierto   8. Cierto

12-10

Answers will vary.

12-11

1. la habitación sencilla / una habitación sencilla / habitación sencilla
2. la recepción / recepción
3. la llave / una llave / llave / la tarjeta magnética / tarjeta magnética / una tarjeta magnética
4. la caja fuerte / una caja fuerte / caja fuerte
5. reservar

12-12

1. e   3. b   5. f   7. c
2. d   4. g   6. a

12-13

1. c　　**2.** b　　**3.** a　　**4.** b　　**5.** a

12-14

1. v, o, a

2. m, a, o

3. p, a, c, a

4. a, a

5. a, p, a, d, u, c, o, c, h

12-15

1. b　　**2.** c　　**3.** a　　**4.** e　　**5.** d

12-19

Answers will vary.

12-20

1. d　　**2.** c　　**3.** b　　**4.** a　　**5.** c

12-21

1. nunca　　　**4.** nada

2. siempre　　　**5.** algo

3. Todos

12-22

1. nunca　　　**4.** nada

2. nunca　　　**5.** nadie

3. ninguna

12-23

1. b　　**2.** e　　**3.** a　　**4.** d　　**5.** c

12-24

Answers will vary.

12-26

1. tenga　　　**4.** ofrezca

2. esté　　　**5.** sirva

3. haya　　　**6.** sea

12-27

1. a　　**2.** b　　**3.** b　　**4.** a　　**5.** b　　**6.** b

12-28

1. b　　**2.** a　　**3.** a　　**4.** b　　**5.** a　　**6.** b

12-29

1. que tenga dos puertas

2. que gaste poca gasolina

3. que tenga aire acondicionado

4. que no sea muy caro

5. que vaya rápido

12-30

1. tienen　　　**4.** dé

2. publican　　　**5.** van

3. tenga

12-31

Answers will vary.

12-32

Answers will vary.

12-34

1. tuyas　　　**4.** nuestros

2. nuestras　　　**5.** suyas / tuyas

3. suyas

12-35

Answers will vary.

12-36

1. la mía　　　**4.** la tuya

2. los tuyos　　　**5.** los suyos

3. la suya

12-37

Answers will vary.

12-38

1. a　　**2.** b　　**3.** c　　**4.** a

12-40

1. b　　　**4.** c

2. a　　　**5.** a

3. a　　　**6.** c

12-41

1. Cierto　　　**3.** Cierto

2. Posible　　　**4.** Improbable

5. Posible

6. Cierto

7. Posible

8. Improbable

12-42

1. Cierto

2. No se menciona

3. Cierto

4. Cierto

5. Falso

6. Falso

7. No se menciona

12-43

1. es

2. haya

3. puedan

4. tenga

5. llevan

6. exista

7. vengan

8. pueden

12-44

1. esté

2. hable

3. pruebe

4. visite

5. encuentre

12-45

1. haya

2. desaparezcan

3. usen

4. vayan

5. anden

6. es

12-46

Answers will vary.

12-50

Answers will vary.

12-51

1. Falso

2. Cierto

3. Falso

4. No se menciona

5. Falso

6. Cierto

7. No se menciona

12-52

Answers will vary.

12-53

1. e

2. c

3. d

4. b

5. g

6. a

7. f

12-54

1. Cierto

2. Cierto

3. Falso

4. Falso

5. Cierto

6. Cierto

7. No se menciona

8. No se menciona

12-55

1. San José

2. Sarchí

3. Irazú

4. Puntarenas

12-56

Answers will vary.

12-57

Answers will vary.

12-58

Answers will vary.

12-60

Answers will vary.

12-61

1. c

2. b

3. a

4. c

5. a

12-62

1. Cierto

2. Falso

3. No se menciona

4. No se menciona

5. Falso

6. Falso

Capítulo 13

13-05

1. a　**2.** d　**3.** b　**4.** e　**5.** c

13-06

1. escritor

2. temas

3. amor

4. amistad

5. desarrollo

6. premios

13-07

1. b　**2.** a　**3.** b　**4.** a　**5.** c

13-08

	¹p	a	i	s	²a	j	e							
					u									
					t									
					o									
					³r	e	c	u	⁴e	r	d	o	s	
		⁵f			r				s					
		o			e				c					
		r			t			⁶c	u	b	i	s	t	a
		⁷m	u	r	a	l		l						
		a			a			t						
		s			t			o						
		o			o			r						

13-09

1. b **2.** a **3.** c **4.** a **5.** c **6.** b

13-10

1. Cierto
2. Falso
3. No se menciona
4. Cierto
5. Cierto
6. No se menciona
7. Cierto

13-11

Answers will vary.

13-12

Selected words: bailarina, escultora, muralista, novelista, pintor, poeta

13-13

1. f **2.** b **3.** d **4.** e **5.** a **6.** c

13-14

1. obra
2. símbolos
3. cuento
4. murales
5. voz
6. novela

13-15

1. cuento / poema
2. poema
3. melodía
4. paisaje
5. mural

13-16

Answers will vary.

13-20

1. E **3.** D **5.** D **7.** D
2. E **4.** E **6.** E

13-21

1. regresé **5.** tenía **9.** nos alojamos
2. Viajé **6.** salí **10.** pasamos
3. estaba **7.** sentí **11.** Fue
4. llegamos **8.** volví

13-22

Answers will vary.

13-23

1. era **5.** visité **9.** gustaba
2. viajaba **6.** era **10.** fue
3. íbamos **7.** visitaba
4. había **8.** pasé

13-24

Answers will vary.

13-26

1. d **2.** c **3.** a **4.** b **5.** e

13-27

1. Carlos **4.** Cecilia **7.** Cecilia
2. Cecilia **5.** Carlos
3. Carlos **6.** ambos

13-28

Answers may vary.

13-29

Answers will vary.

13-30

Answers will vary.

13-32

1. a   **2.** b   **3.** c   **4.** a   **5.** a

13-33

1. se conocieron

2. se veían

3. se escribían, se llamaban

4. se querían

5. se abrazaron / se besaron, se besaron / se abrazaron

13-34

Answers will vary.

13-35

Answers may vary.

13-39

Selected words: cuento, ensayo, novela, poema

13-40

1. Cierto   **5.** Falso

2. Falso   **6.** Cierto

3. Cierto   **7.** No se menciona

4. No se menciona

13-41

Answers will vary.

13-42

Answers will vary.

13-43

b

13-44

Answers will vary.

13-45

1. 1955   **2.** 1972   **3.** 1974

13-46

Answers will vary.

13-47

Answers will vary.

13-49

1. b   **2.** b   **3.** b   **4.** c   **5.** d

13-50

Answers will vary.

13-51

1. Cierto   **5.** Cierto

2. Cierto   **6.** Cierto

3. No se menciona   **7.** Falso

4. Falso

13-52

1. c   **2.** b   **3.** b   **4.** a   **5.** c   **6.** c

Capítulo 14

14-05

1. b   **2.** c   **3.** d   **4.** e   **5.** a   **6.** f

14-06

alta esperanza de vida, democracia, derechos, diversificación,

14-07

1. tasa   **4.** políglotas

2. derechos   **5.** mortalidad

3. se ha destacado   **6.** drogas

14-08

Answers will vary.

14-09

1. Falso   **5.** Falso

2. Cierto   **6.** Falso

3. Falso   **7.** Cierto

4. No se menciona   **8.** No se menciona

14-10

1. a   **2.** c   **3.** b   **4.** a   **5.** b

14-11

1. Cierto
2. Cierto
3. No se menciona
4. Cierto
5. Falso
6. Cierto
7. No se menciona

14-12

Answers will vary.

14-13

1. d
2. e
3. a
4. b
5. c

14-14

1. económica
2. En vez de
3. emigrar
4. proximidad
5. adaptación

14-18

1. c
2. e
3. b
4. a
5. d

14-19

1. a
2. c
3. b
4. a
5. b

14-20

1. tenga
2. podamos
3. vendas
4. estudien
5. sepa

14-21

1. nos casemos
2. hagas
3. laves
4. trabajes
5. saques

14-22

Answers will vary.

14-24

1. conozca
2. encuentre
3. ganemos
4. me gradúe
5. quiera
6. me establezca

14-25

1. a
2. a
3. b
4. b
5. b

14-26

1. prefiero
2. me levanto
3. desayuno
4. llego
5. diga
6. cierra

7. llego
8. haya
9. terminan
10. hablamos

14-27

1. termine
2. pueda
3. reciba
4. llegue
5. existe

14-28

1. b
2. b
3. a
4. a

14-30

1. antes de la universidad
2. antes de la universidad
3. en la universidad
4. en la universidad
5. antes de la universidad

14-31

Answers will vary.

14-32

1. había buscado
2. había leído
3. había entrevistado
4. había consultado
5. había encontrado

14-33

1. había viajado
2. había participado
3. había manejado
4. había recibido
5. había hecho

14-34

Answers will vary.

14-36

Answers will vary.

14-37

Answers will vary.

14-38

Answers will vary.

14-39

1. No fumar
2. No nadar
3. No estacionar
4. No hablar
5. No tocar

14-40

Answers will vary.

14-44

Selected words: emigración, esperanza de vida, migración, mortalidad, población, tasa

14-45

1. Cierto
2. Falso
3. No se menciona
4. Cierto
5. Cierto
6. No se menciona
7. Falso

14-46

Answers will vary.

14-47

Answers will vary.

14-48

Answers will vary.

14-49

1. b   2. c   3. c

14-50

1. Falso
2. No se menciona
3. Cierto
4. No se menciona
5. Cierto
6. Cierto
7. Cierto
8. Falso

14-51

Answers will vary.

14-52

Answers will vary.

14-54

1. trate
2. salir
3. alcancen
4. tengan
5. reciban

14-55

1. a   2. b   3. a   4. c

14-56

Answers will vary.

Capítulo 15

15-05

Selected words: acceso, biblioteca digital, buscador, enlace, mensaje

15-06

1. acceso
2. intercambio
3. mensaje
4. enlace
5. adjunto
6. diseminación
7. videojuegos

15-07

1. c   2. d   3. b   4. a

15-08

1. b   2. d   3. c   4. d   5. a

15-09

Selected words: el bosque tropical, la capa de ozono, la deforestación, la extinción, la tierra

15-10

1. c   2. e   3. d   4. b   5. f   6. a

15-11

1. No se menciona
2. Falso
3. Cierto
4. Cierto
5. No se menciona
6. Cierto

15-12

Answers will vary.

15-13

1. a   3. b   5. a   7. a
2. c   4. c   6. b

15-14

1. f   2. b   3. d   4. a   5. e   6. c

15-15

Answers may vary.

15-16

Answers will vary.

15-20

1. comiera
2. hiciera
3. jugara
4. viera
5. visitara
6. fuera

15-21

1. es
2. tiene
3. tengan
4. haya
5. tengan

15-22

1. sentara
2. cambiara
3. fuéramos
4. pasáramos
5. visitáramos
6. pagara
7. cancelara

15-23

1. quisiera
2. conociera
3. visitaran
4. perdiera
5. fueran
6. se perdieran
7. comieran
8. fuera

15-24

1. hiciera
2. conociera
3. tuviera
4. escuchara
5. me divirtiera

15-25

1. estudiáramos
2. fuera
3. ganara, viniera
4. saliera
5. vinieras

15-26

1. Habla como si fuera inteligente / Habla como si fuera muy inteligente
2. Habla como si entendiera nuestros problemas
3. Habla como si conociera a nuestro presidente / Habla como si conociera al presidente
4. Habla como si quisiera ser nuestro amigo / Habla como si fuera nuestro amigo / Habla como si quisiera ser amigo nuestro / Habla como si fuera amigo nuestro

15-28

1. se acabarán
2. hablaré
3. trabajamos
4. haces
5. contribuiré
6. se resolverán

15-29

1. c   2. e   3. a   4. d   5. b

15-30

1. aceptaré
2. estaría
3. tendría
4. usaré
5. conseguiré
6. me quedaría

15-31

1. b   2. a   3. b   4. a   5. c

15-32

Answers will vary.

15-33

Answers will vary.

15-34

Answers will vary.

15-36

1. 2   2. 3   3. 1   4. 4

15-37

1. a Manuel
2. a ti
3. a Vanessa y a Manuel
4. a Vanessa
5. a Vanessa y a ti
6. a Vanessa

15-38

1. cayó
2. olvidaron
3. perdieron
4. acabó
5. quedó

15-39

1. Y a mí se me cayó el papel / Y se me cayó el papel a mí / A mí se me cayó el papel / Se me cayó el papel a mí

2. Y a mí se me rompió la calculadora / Y se me rompió la calculadora a mí / A mí se me rompió la calculadora / Se me rompió la calculadora a mí

3. Y a mí se me perdieron los cuadernos / Y se me perdieron los cuadernos a mí / A mí se me perdieron los cuadernos / Se me perdieron los cuadernos a mí

4. Y a mí se me descompuso la computadora / Y se me descompuso la computadora a mí / A mí se me descompuso la computadora / Se me descompuso la computadora a mí

5. Y a mí se me olvidaron las tareas / Y se me olvidaron las tareas a mí / A mí se me olvidaron las tareas / Se me olvidaron las tareas a mí

15-40

Answers will vary.

15-44

Answers will vary.

15-45

1. Falso
2. No se menciona
3. Cierto
4. Cierto
5. Cierto
6. Falso

15-46

1. b   2. c   3. d   4. a

15-47

Answers will vary.

15-48

Answers will vary.

15-49

1. Falso
2. Cierto
3. No se menciona
4. No se menciona
5. Falso
6. Falso
7. No se menciona

15-50

Answers will vary.

15-51

Answers will vary.

15-52

Answers will vary.

15-54

Answers will vary.

15-55

1. librería
2. correo electrónico
3. celular / teléfono / teléfono celular
4. comunicarse
5. cámara

15-56

1. Falso
2. Cierto
3. Cierto
4. No se menciona
5. Falso
6. No se menciona
7. Cierto